LEARN A LOT
WHILE YOU SIT ON
THE POT

"Where potty time meets brain power!"

Dedication & Introduction

To everyone who's ever needed a laugh, learned a fun fact, or solved a riddle while sitting on the throne—this book is for you.

Welcome to "Learn A Lot While You Sit On The Pot"—your ultimate potty companion! Whether you're here for some giggles, a bit of trivia, or a quick brain-teasing challenge, you're in the right place.

Think of this book as the perfect excuse to take a little extra time for yourself (don't worry, we won't tell). So, sit back, relax, and let's make your bathroom breaks both fun and informative.

Remember: learning happens everywhere—even here!

"Happy reading, and don't forget to flush!"

FLUSHES
THROUGH TIME

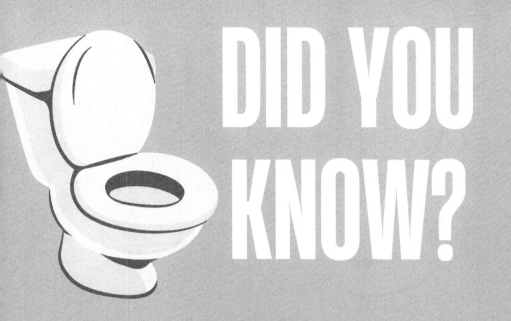

DID YOU KNOW?

In ancient Rome, public toilets called latrinae were communal spaces where people shared sponges on sticks instead of toilet paper! Hygiene wasn't quite what it is today.

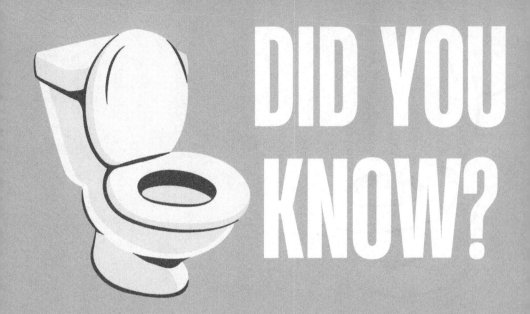

DID YOU KNOW?

King Louis XIV of France often held court meetings while seated on his portable golden throne—a fancy chamber pot!

DID YOU KNOW?

The flushing toilet was invented by Sir John Harington in 1596, but it didn't catch on until centuries later. Harington even installed one for Queen Elizabeth I!

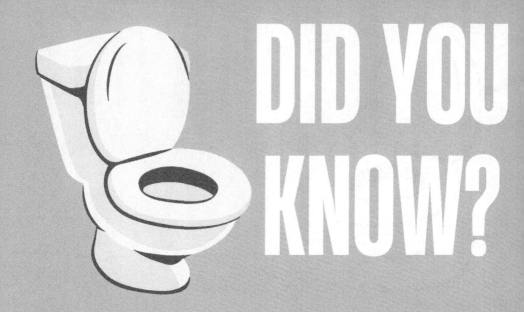

DID YOU KNOW?

Viking settlements often used moss and sheep wool as toilet paper. Talk about resourcefulness!

DID YOU KNOW?

NASA invented a space toilet that suctions waste away in zero gravity. Astronauts even wear "Maximum Absorbency Garments" for long missions!

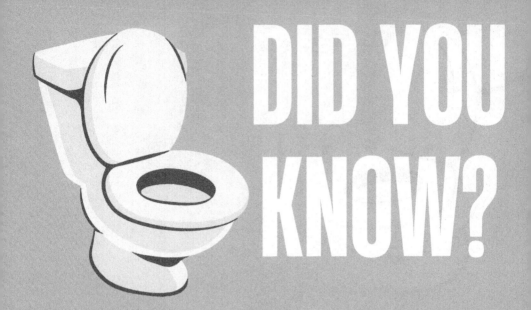

DID YOU KNOW?

In the Middle Ages, castles had "garderobes," where waste fell into moats below. The name suggests it also doubled as a closet for clothes, as the smell deterred moths!

DID YOU KNOW?

In 19th-century London, public toilets called "public conveniences" were marked with gas lamps that had a red light for women and green light for men.

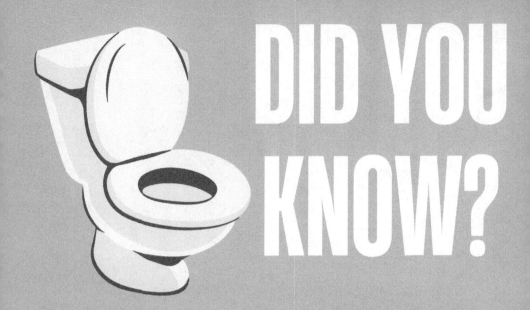

DID YOU KNOW?

Ancient Chinese used bamboo sticks known as chü ts'e as an early form of toilet hygiene—far from soft, but it did the job!

DID YOU KNOW?

The first modern public restroom was installed in 1851 at London's Crystal Palace Exhibition. Attendees paid a penny to use it, coining the term "spend a penny."

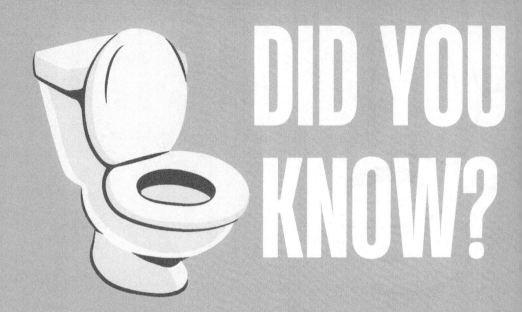

DID YOU KNOW?

The Great Stink of 1858 in London, caused by the River Thames being full of human waste, led to the creation of modern sewers by engineer Joseph Bazalgette.

WILD WASTE WONDERS

Weird and Fun Animal Facts About Poo

 Wombats are famous for their cube-shaped poo, which helps prevent it from rolling away as they use it to mark their territory.

 Penguins can project their poo up to four feet away, thanks to the high pressure in their digestive systems!

 Dung beetles can roll balls of poop up to 50 times their own body weight, making them one of nature's strongest creatures.

 Baby koalas eat their mother's poop (called pap) to get the bacteria needed to digest eucalyptus leaves.

 Rabbits eat their poo (called cecotropes) to redigest nutrients they missed the first time around.

 Pandas can produce up to 40 pounds of poo in a single day due to their bamboo-heavy diet.

Weird and Fun Animal Facts About Poo

	Hippos use their tails to fling their poo, spreading it around to mark their territory.
	Whale poop, rich in nutrients, helps sustain ocean ecosystems by fertilizing phytoplankton, which supports the entire marine food chain.
	Bat droppings, or guano, are so nutrient-rich that they've been used as fertilizer and even in explosives during wartime.
	Elephant dung contains so much fiber that it can be turned into eco-friendly paper, a sustainable product in many countries.
	Sloths only poop about once a week, and when they do, they climb down from their trees, making them vulnerable to predators.
	Termites use their poop, a sticky and durable material, to build their elaborate mounds and tunnels, which can last for decades!

Weird and Fun Animal Facts About Poo

 Some frogs turn their stomachs inside out to "vomit" harmful food, then swallow them back once clean!

 During winter, bees hold in their waste for weeks or months, waiting for a warm enough day to take a "cleansing flight" outside the hive.

 When threatened, sea cucumbers can eject their intestines (along with some waste) at predators. They later regenerate the lost organs!

 Lemurs will pee on their hands and then rub it on tree branches to mark their territory and send messages to other lemurs.

 Parrotfish eat coral and poop out sand, creating beautiful beaches in tropical areas.

 In cold climates, penguins poop in their burrows to generate heat and keep their nests warm.

Weird and Fun Animal Facts About Poo

	Researchers study pangolin poop to understand their diets and trace their habitats in the wild.
	Geckos leave their droppings in prominent spots to mark their territory and ward off rivals.
	Capybaras use communal pooping spots, and their waste releases scents to communicate within their group.
	Pistol shrimps release bursts of bubbles and poop into the water to mark their burrows and claim territory.
	Some caterpillars can shoot their poop up to six feet away to avoid detection by predators!
	Hyenas use communal latrines to leave "messages" in their poop, communicating social status and territorial boundaries.

Weird and Fun Animal Facts About Poo

 Some freshwater turtles cover themselves in poop from other animals to hide from predators.

 Some snails eat their own poop to reabsorb calcium for their shells!

 Manatee poop provides nutrients to help seagrass beds thrive, essential for underwater ecosystems.

 Civets eat coffee cherries and poop out the seeds, which are used to make the expensive "kopi luwak" coffee.

 Clams filter water and release nutrient-rich poop, which helps maintain clean aquatic environments.

 Lizard droppings often contain white tips, made of uric acid, helping scientists identify them in the wild.

Riddle Me This

I'm a seat where you take a rest,
And after you're done, you flush the mess. What
am I?

_____

I'm soft, I'm rolled, I'm easy to tear,
I'm a bathroom staple everywhere. What am I?

_____

I twist, I turn, I splash, I spin,
Down goes everything within. What am I?

_____

Answer 1	Answer 2	Answer 3
A toilet	Toilet paper	A toilet flush

Riddle Me This

I'm small and round, and on a stick I roll,
A beetle like me loves digging a hole. What am I?

_____

I'm square but not for sitting,
I mark the spot where a wombat's been hitting.
What am I?

_____

I'm the sound you don't want when you're done,
If I keep running, it's not much fun. What am I?

_____

Answer 1	Answer 2	Answer 3
A dung beetle	Wombat poop	A leaky toilet

Riddle Me This

I'm tall, brown, and often found,
Dropping plops to the ground. What am I?

_____

I'm a colorful roll of the scented kind,
But too fancy, and no one will find. What am I?

_____

I have a tank, but no army,
I'm in your home but not the pantry. What am I?

_____

Answer 1	Answer 2	Answer 3
A giraffe (pooping)	Decorative toilet paper	A toilet tank

Riddle Me This

I'm a pit in the ground, deep and wide,
In olden days, that's where waste would hide. What am I?

_____

I'm flushed and gone,
But in a sewer, I travel on. What am I?

_____

I start as food and end as waste,
In the middle, I'm a digestive race. What am I?

_____

Answer 1	Answer 2	Answer 3
A latrine	Wastewater	Poop

Riddle Me This

I'm used by astronauts, far from home,
Suction keeps me in my zone. What am I?

I'm soft, furry, and sometimes smelly,
My droppings make fertilizer for your veggie belly.
What am I?

You'll find me in a bottle or near a throne,
When you spray me, bad smells are gone. What am I?

Answer 1	Answer 2	Answer 3
A space toilet	A rabbit	Air freshener

Riddle Me This

In some cultures, I'm made of gold,
Sit on me and feel bold! What am I?

_____

I keep it clean and sparkling bright,
With a swirl and some foam, I'm out of sight. What
am I?

_____

I'm used for aiming, keeping it neat,
A little fly decal at your feet. What am I?

_____

Answer 1   Answer 2   Answer 3
A golden toilet   Toilet cleaner   A urinal fly target

Riddle Me This

I'm a bucket with a hole,
In some places, I'm the toilet's role. What am I?

———————————

I'm the place where public goes,
Coins for entry—watch your toes! What am I?

———————————

I hold the roll,
But I'm not whole. What am I?

———————————

Answer 1

A chamber pot

Answer 2

A pay toilet

Answer 3

A toilet paper holder

Riddle Me This

I bubble, fizz, and sometimes hiss,
Cleaning toilets is my bliss. What am I?

_____

I'm often called a throne,
But I'm no king, just porcelain. What am I?

_____

I'm a lever or button you press,
Without me, things would make a mess. What am I?

_____

Answer 1	Answer 2	Answer 3
Toilet tablets	A toilet	A flush handle

Riddle Me This

I take your waste far away,
Pipes lead me out day by day. What am I?

———————

I'm a fluffy seat for those who care,
A cozy touch that's soft and rare. What am I?

———————

I'm sometimes blue and sometimes pink,
I make water fresher than you think. What am I?

———————

Answer 1	Answer 2	Answer 3
A sewer system	A toilet seat cover	Toilet bowl cleaner tablets

Riddle Me This

I'm the restroom game that keeps you bright,
Grab me and learn while in the light. What am I?

———————

I'm the sound of a flop or a plop,
But once I'm in, I'll never stop. What am I?

———————

I'm the tool that unclogs the goo,
Push and pull, it's what I do. What am I?

———————

Answer 1	Answer 2	Answer 3
A toilet trivia book	Something falling into the toilet	A plunger

FLUSHY BRAIN TEASERS

Toilet
— LOGIC PUZZLES —

If toilet paper rolls are best kept on a holder, and plungers are best kept near the toilet, where's the best place for a bathroom book?

(On a shelf.)

If poop is number two, and pee is number one, what happens when you combine one and two?

(You get three—or a really long bathroom break!)

Toilet
LOGIC PUZZLES

If a toilet flushes clockwise in the Northern Hemisphere, and counterclockwise in the Southern Hemisphere, how does it flush at the equator?

(It flushes straight down!)

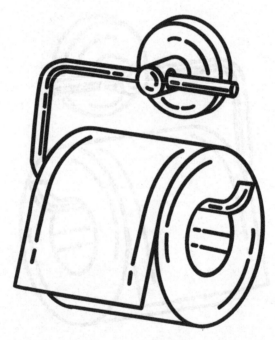

If a bathroom has two rolls of toilet paper, but one is empty, what's left?

(A bad situation—or just one roll!)

Toilet
LOGIC PUZZLES

If a penguin's poo shoots 4 feet, and a hippo's tail flings it in all directions, what happens if they share a bathroom?

(A messy masterpiece!)

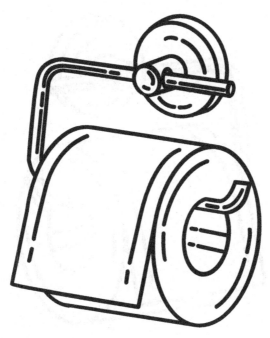

If a bidet sprays and toilet paper wipes, what cleans up better in a flood?

(Neither—they both go down the drain!)

Toilet
LOGIC PUZZLES

If a plunger is used to unclog a toilet, and soap is used to clean hands, what tool is used to fix a leaky pipe?

(A wrench—or a plumber!)

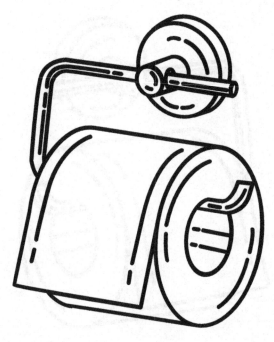

If a toilet can flush 3 gallons per flush, how many flushes does it take to fill a 15-gallon tank?

(Five flushes.)

Toilet
LOGIC PUZZLES

If wombat poop is cube-shaped and rabbit poop is round, what's the shape of a perfect poo?

(Whatever makes you happy—it's subjective!)

If a poop emoji is made of chocolate and a real one isn't, what do they both have in common?

(They're both a conversation starter!)

POTTY
PUNCHLINES

WHY DID THE TOILET BREAK UP WITH THE SINK?

Because it felt drained!

WHAT DO YOU CALL A FAIRY WHO FIXES TOILETS?

Stinker Bell!

WHY DON'T TOILETS EVER GET INTO ARGUMENTS?

Because they just let things go!

WHY DID THE PLUMBER BRING A PENCIL TO THE BATHROOM?

To draw water!

WHAT DID ONE TOILET SAY TO THE OTHER?

"you look flushed!"

WHY DID THE TOILET PAPER REFUSE TO CROSS THE ROAD?

It didn't want to get stuck in a crack!

WHAT'S A TOILET'S FAVORITE GAME?

Hide-and-go-flush!

WHY WAS THE MATH BOOK SAD IN THE BATHROOM?

It had too many problems to solve!

WHAT DO YOU CALL A MUSICAL TOILET?

Flush gordon!

WHY DID THE TOILET REFUSE TO PLAY CARDS?

It was tired of getting a flush every time!

WHAT'S A PLUMBER'S FAVORITE KIND OF MUSIC?

Pipe tunes!

WHAT DID THE TOILET SAY TO THE PLUNGER?

"You're my number one tool!"

WHY DO TOILETS HATE SURPRISES?

They like to know what's coming down the pipeline!

WHAT DO ASTRONAUTS CALL THEIR SPACE TOILET?

The Pee-pee Pod!

WHY DID THE TOILET PAPER START A BAND?

Because it was on a roll!

WHAT'S A TOILET'S LEAST FAVORITE EXERCISE?

Squats!

WHY DID THE PORTABLE TOILET GET PROMOTED?

It was outstanding in its field!

WHAT'S THE BEST WAY TO FIX A BROKEN TOILET?

With a flush of inspiration!

WHY DON'T TOILETS GOSSIP?

Because they keep everything private!

WHY DID THE TOILET WIN THE RACE?

Because it was the fastest thing in the bowl!

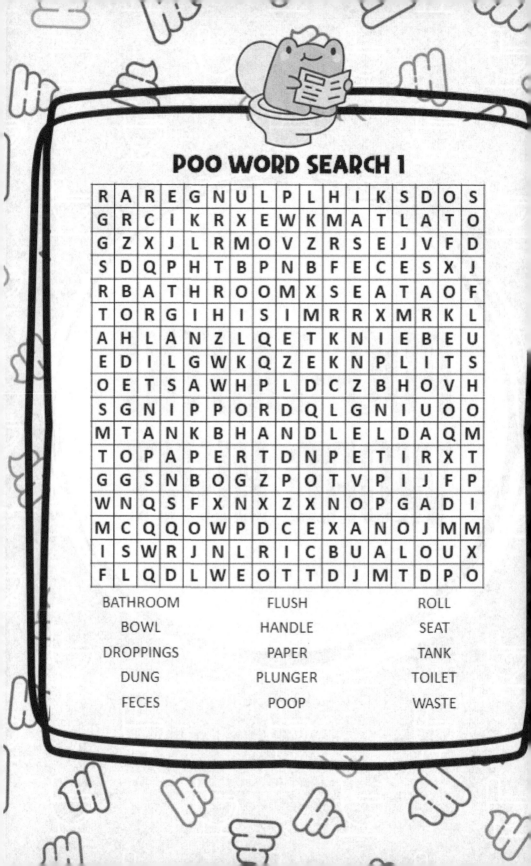

POO WORD SEARCH 1

R	A	R	E	G	N	U	L	P	L	H	I	K	S	D	O	S
G	R	C	I	K	R	X	E	W	K	M	A	T	L	A	T	O
G	Z	X	J	L	R	M	O	V	Z	R	S	E	J	V	F	D
S	D	Q	P	H	T	B	P	N	B	F	E	C	E	S	X	J
R	B	A	T	H	R	O	O	M	X	S	E	A	T	A	O	F
T	O	R	G	I	H	I	S	I	M	R	R	X	M	R	K	L
A	H	L	A	N	Z	L	Q	E	T	K	N	I	E	B	E	U
E	D	I	L	G	W	K	Q	Z	E	K	N	P	L	I	T	S
O	E	T	S	A	W	H	P	L	D	C	Z	B	H	O	V	H
S	G	N	I	P	P	O	R	D	Q	L	G	N	I	U	O	O
M	T	A	N	K	B	H	A	N	D	L	E	L	D	A	Q	M
T	O	P	A	P	E	R	T	D	N	P	E	T	I	R	X	T
G	G	S	N	B	O	G	Z	P	O	T	V	P	I	J	F	P
W	N	Q	S	F	X	N	X	Z	X	N	O	P	G	A	D	I
M	C	Q	Q	O	W	P	D	C	E	X	A	N	O	J	M	M
I	S	W	R	J	N	L	R	I	C	B	U	A	L	O	U	X
F	L	Q	D	L	W	E	O	T	T	D	J	M	T	D	P	O

BATHROOM	FLUSH	ROLL
BOWL	HANDLE	SEAT
DROPPINGS	PAPER	TANK
DUNG	PLUNGER	TOILET
FECES	POOP	WASTE

POO WORD SEARCH 2

A	E	J	D	L	X	D	V	J	M	I	F	Z	X	D	U	K
S	Z	A	V	W	O	L	X	C	V	T	X	J	V	P	D	K
K	J	U	U	P	L	O	H	U	G	F	N	L	N	I	E	X
U	Q	V	L	O	W	C	T	M	S	Q	R	C	H	M	F	C
Q	S	T	O	Z	C	L	U	S	G	A	O	S	G	O	E	T
L	U	C	U	R	V	E	A	M	E	L	U	W	G	B	C	R
N	Z	T	R	K	E	A	M	G	O	R	Z	Z	C	N	A	A
F	R	S	S	L	P	N	L	N	B	G	G	F	S	S	T	F
C	C	E	S	O	K	Q	K	O	K	X	L	F	M	L	E	E
J	T	G	C	R	A	U	O	K	O	G	Z	C	E	H	U	I
T	J	I	D	V	B	P	T	G	C	P	B	W	I	M	F	E
U	P	D	Z	O	J	B	Q	E	A	V	O	P	C	R	I	B
X	T	O	D	V	W	U	O	D	D	B	F	T	D	W	S	S
E	E	D	N	I	H	P	R	U	T	I	W	N	D	Z	B	E
B	P	J	E	N	S	T	I	N	K	S	B	M	H	S	A	W
D	I	A	P	Z	E	T	E	R	C	X	E	E	J	M	U	G
W	W	C	O	W	O	C	B	F	K	P	P	G	R	D	F	X

BIDET	DEFECATE	SOAP
BOWEL	DIGEST	STINK
BRUSH	EXCRETE	STOOL
CLEAN	FART	WASH
COLON	LOO	WIPE

POO WORD SEARCH 3

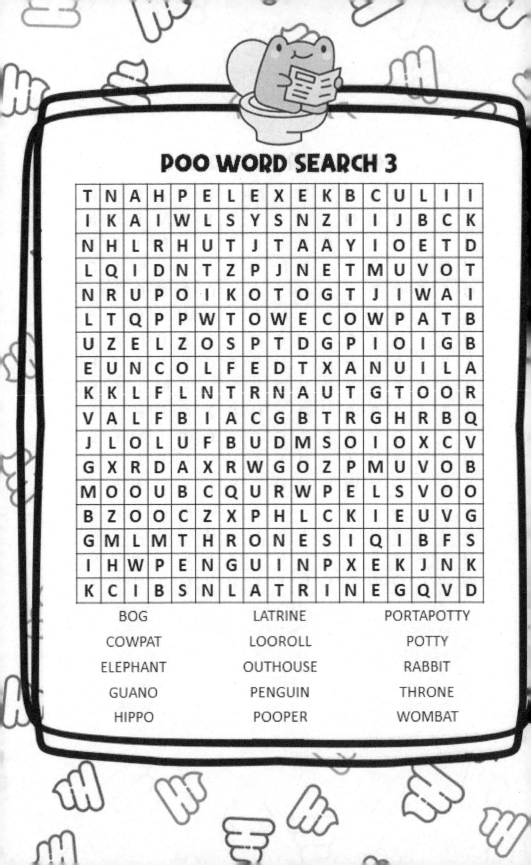

T	N	A	H	P	E	L	E	X	E	K	B	C	U	L	I	I
I	K	A	I	W	L	S	Y	S	N	Z	I	I	J	B	C	K
N	H	L	R	H	U	T	J	T	A	A	Y	I	O	E	T	D
L	Q	I	D	N	T	Z	P	J	N	E	T	M	U	V	O	T
N	R	U	P	O	I	K	O	T	O	G	T	J	I	W	A	I
L	T	Q	P	P	W	T	O	W	E	C	O	W	P	A	T	B
U	Z	E	L	Z	O	S	P	T	D	G	P	I	O	I	G	B
E	U	N	C	O	L	F	E	D	T	X	A	N	U	I	L	A
K	K	L	F	L	N	T	R	N	A	U	T	G	T	O	O	R
V	A	L	F	B	I	A	C	G	B	T	R	G	H	R	B	Q
J	L	O	L	U	F	B	U	D	M	S	O	I	O	X	C	V
G	X	R	D	A	X	R	W	G	O	Z	P	M	U	V	O	B
M	O	O	U	B	C	Q	U	R	W	P	E	L	S	V	O	O
B	Z	O	O	C	Z	X	P	H	L	C	K	I	E	U	V	G
G	M	L	M	T	H	R	O	N	E	S	I	Q	I	B	F	S
I	H	W	P	E	N	G	U	I	N	P	X	E	K	J	N	K
K	C	I	B	S	N	L	A	T	R	I	N	E	G	Q	V	D

BOG	LATRINE	PORTAPOTTY
COWPAT	LOOROLL	POTTY
ELEPHANT	OUTHOUSE	RABBIT
GUANO	PENGUIN	THRONE
HIPPO	POOPER	WOMBAT

POO WORD SEARCH 1 (SOLUTION)

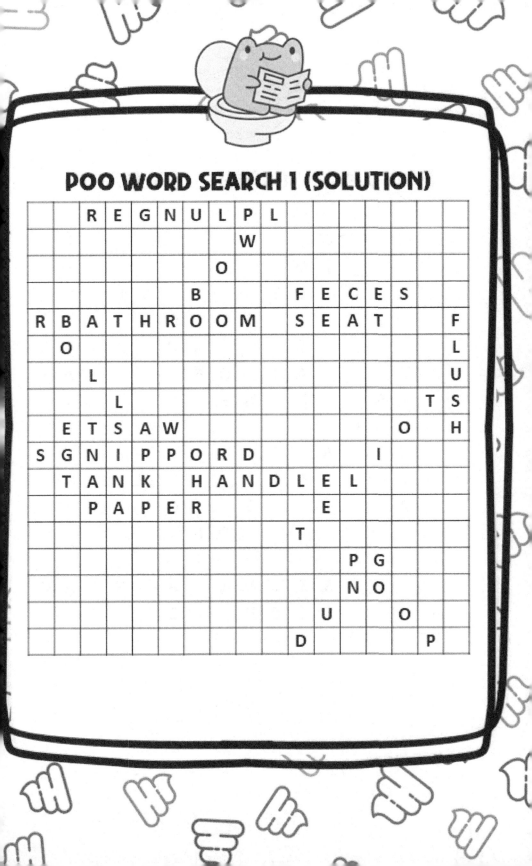

		R	E	G	N	U	L	P	L						
							W								
						O									
				B				F	E	C	E	S			
R	B	A	T	H	R	O	O	M	S	E	A	T			F
	O														L
	L														U
		L											T	S	
	E	T	S	A	W							O		H	
S	G	N	I	P	P	O	R	D			I				
	T	A	N	K		H	A	N	D	L	E	L			
	P	A	P	E	R				E						
							T								
								P	G						
								N	O						
							U			O					
							D			P					

POO WORD SEARCH 2 (SOLUTION)

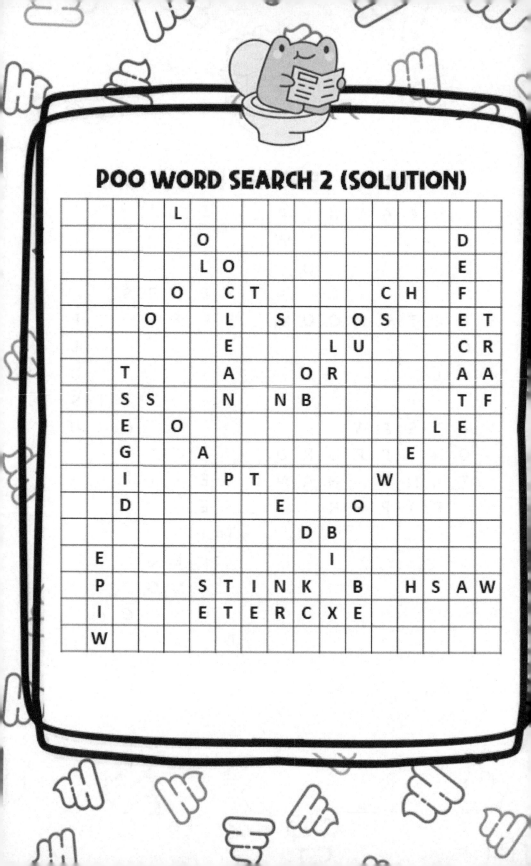

			L												
				O									D		
				L		O							E		
				O		C	T				C	H	F		
			O			L		S			O	S	E	T	
						E			L	U			C	R	
		T				A		O	R				A	A	
		S	S			N		N	B				T	F	
		E		O								L	E		
		G			A					E					
		I			P	T			W						
		D				E		O							
						D	B								
	E						I								
	P			S	T	I	N	K		B		H	S	A	W
	I			E	T	E	R	C	X	E					
	W														

POO WORD SEARCH 3 (SOLUTION)

T	N	A	H	P	E	L	E	E							
								Y							
	H				T					Y					
		I		T	P					T					T
			P	O	P					T					I
			P	P	P				C	O	W	P	A	T	B
				O	P					P		O			B
				O	E		T			A		U			A
	L			N	R		A			T		T			R
	L				A		B			R		H			
	O				U		M			O		O			
	R					G	O			P		U			B
	O						W					S			O
	O											E			G
	L		T	H	R	O	N	E							
		P	E	N	G	U	I	N							
				L	A	T	R	I	N	E					

LOO LORE AND MORE

FUN BATHROOM FACTS

TOILET PAPER'S FIRST AD

The first-ever toilet paper advertisement in 1880 called it a "medicated paper" to avoid embarrassment about its real use.

FIRST HEATED TOILET SEATS

Heated toilet seats were introduced in Japan in the 1980s and have become a global trend for comfort.

THE TOILET PAPER SHORTAGE PANIC

In 1973, a joke by a comedian about a toilet paper shortage caused mass panic, leading to actual shortages in stores.

THE TALLEST TOILET

A luxury hotel in Dubai has a toilet on the 154th floor, the highest above-ground toilet in the world!

FUN BATHROOM FACTS

THE AVERAGE TOILET LIFESPAN

A standard toilet can last over 50 years with proper maintenance, outliving most home appliances.

TOILETS IN LITERATURE

The first mention of a flushing toilet in fiction was in Gulliver's Travels (1726) by Jonathan Swift.

TOILET SEAT MYTHS

Toilet seats are often thought to be the germiest place in the bathroom, but sinks and doorknobs typically host more bacteria.

THE ROYAL FLUSH ORIGIN

The term "royal flush" in card games comes from the 16th-century practice of calling royal palaces "flush houses" after they installed flushing toilets.

FUN BATHROOM FACTS

TOILET MUSEUMS EXIST

India is home to the Sulabh International Museum of Toilets, showcasing toilets from ancient to modern times.

TOILETS IN TV HISTORY

The first toilet ever shown on TV was in the sitcom Leave It to Beaver in 1957—though only the tank was visible!

BATHROOM BREAK RECORD

Astronaut Alan Shepard took the longest "bathroom break" in history—holding it for 8 hours during his Mercury space mission in 1961.

GOLDEN THRONES IN HISTORY

King Louis XIV of France famously held court while on his portable toilet, believing it showed power and efficiency.

FUN BATHROOM FACTS

TOILETS AND TIME

The average person spends about 3 years of their life on the toilet!

URINALS WITH TARGETS

Some urinals in Amsterdam have tiny painted flies in the bowl to improve aim and reduce cleaning.

ECO-TOILETS IN HISTORY

Ancient Chinese toilets used soil and ash to compost waste long before modern eco-toilet designs were created.

TOILETS IN VIDEO GAMES

Toilets have been hidden Easter eggs in games like The Sims and Doom, showing their cultural significance.

FUN BATHROOM FACTS

TOILET BREAK LAWS

In the UK, it's illegal for employers to prevent workers from using the toilet during work hours.

PORTABLE TOILET INVENTION

The first portable toilet was invented in the 1940s for dock workers, made of wood and a small tank.

TOILET-THEMED RESTAURANTS

There are restaurants in Taiwan where diners sit on toilet seats and eat from bowl-shaped dishes—yes, really!

LONGEST PEE RECORD

The world record for the longest continuous pee is 508 seconds (about 8.5 minutes), set by a man in Belgium!

RHYMES ON
THE THRONE

Soap in hand, I take the stage,
The shower curtain hides my age.

Steam and water set the mood,
My bathroom fans are so subdued.

I sing of love, I sing of pain,
I'd tour the world, but there's the drain.

So every night, my concert's clear,
Just me, my soap, and shampoo near!

Look in the mirror, what do you see?
Wash those hands, let germs flee!

Some read books, some just sit,
Either way, it's a perfect fit!

Soft and strong, I'm always near,
I'm the friend you hold most dear!

Soap and bubbles, steam and foam,
This is my happy, watery home!

I hang around, day by day,
Waiting for hands to pull me away.

Soft and fluffy, strong and neat,
A bathroom's best friend, so hard to beat.

Over or under, I won't take sides,
Just roll me out, I'll be your guide.

And when I'm gone, don't shed a tear,
A new roll's waiting, always near!

I sit in silence, cold and white,
A porcelain throne both day and night.

From mighty flush to gentle swirl,
I welcome all—boy, girl, or squirrel!

So take a seat, don't be shy,
I'm here for you, just give me a try.

But please remember, when you're done,
A little flush is always fun!

Around the bend and down the pipe,
Through twists and turns of every type.

A watery world, both dark and deep,
Where all the flushed go for their sleep.

To sewers vast or treatment plants,
It's quite a journey (not for pants!).

So next time you pull that lever down,
Imagine the trip beneath your town!

Knock before you open the door,
Privacy's sacred, need I say more?

Don't hog the space, don't make a mess,
A tidy bathroom's the key to success.

Flush it down, don't leave a trace,
And always clean the mirror's face.

If you follow these rules, you'll never fear,
A sparkling loo is always near!

I'm often ignored, but I'm quite the treat,
A little fountain for your seat.

With a gentle spray, I do my best,
To leave you clean and feeling blessed.

No need for paper, no need for waste,
Just water magic, pure and chaste.

So if you see me, give me a try,
I'm the bidet—don't pass me by!

A tub of bubbles, warm and deep,
Where worries drift and dreams can leap.

Candles flicker, scents arise,
A perfect place for closed eyes.

Splish and splash, the stress is gone,
Sing a tune or hum a song.

For when the day has been too tough,
A bubble bath is just enough!

FLUSH-FRIENDLY HEALTH TIPS

FUN
HEALTH TIPS

An apple a day keeps constipation away!

TiP

Apples are full of fiber and water, helping keep things moving smoothly.

FUN
HEALTH TIPS

Sip, sip, hooray!

TiP

Drinking water regularly can prevent dehydration and keep your digestive system happy.

FUN
HEALTH TIPS

Beans, beans,
they're good for your heart—and your gut!

TiP

Beans are high in fiber, promoting healthy digestion and regularity.

FUN
HEALTH TIPS

Stay juicy with fruits!

TiP

Fruits like oranges, pears, and watermelon hydrate you while providing natural fiber.

FUN
HEALTH TIPS

H2O is the way to go!

TIP

Water helps soften stool and prevent digestive discomfort.

FUN
HEALTH TIPS

Chew your greens for happy bowels!

TiP

Leafy vegetables like spinach and kale are fiber-packed powerhouses for digestion.

FUN
HEALTH TIPS

Popcorn for the win!

TiP

Air-popped popcorn is a tasty, fiber-rich snack that supports a healthy gut.

FUN
HEALTH TIPS

Berries bring the fiber fun!

TiP

Raspberries and blackberries are loaded with fiber to keep things flowing naturally.

FUN
HEALTH TIPS

Cucumbers are cool for digestion!

TiP

With high water content and fiber, cucumbers keep you hydrated and regular.

FUN
HEALTH TIPS

Nuts about digestion!

TiP

Almonds and walnuts add fiber, protein, and healthy fats for overall gut health.

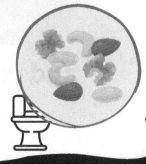

Now that you've finished your business, flush it clean

wipe it bright

and we'll see you next time, alright?

Made in the USA
Coppell, TX
17 December 2024